ESSENTIAL LIBRARY OF
THE US MILITARY
★ THE US ★
COAST GUARD

Essential Library

An Imprint of Abdo Publishing | www.abdopublishing.com

ESSENTIAL LIBRARY OF
THE US MILITARY

★ THE US ★
COAST GUARD

BY KRISTIN MARCINIAK

CONTENT CONSULTANT
CAPTAIN GLENN SULMASY
CHAIRMAN, DEPARTMENT OF HUMANITIES
UNITED STATES COAST GUARD ACADEMY

www.abdopublishing.com

Published by Abdo Publishing, a division of ABDO, PO Box 398166, Minneapolis, Minnesota 55439. Copyright © 2015 by Abdo Consulting Group, Inc. International copyrights reserved in all countries. No part of this book may be reproduced in any form without written permission from the publisher. Essential Library™ is a trademark and logo of Abdo Publishing.

Printed in the United States of America, North Mankato, Minnesota
042014
092014

THIS BOOK CONTAINS
RECYCLED MATERIALS

Cover Photo: US Coast Guard
Interior Photos: US Coast Guard, 2, 9, 11, 17, 31, 33, 36–37, 40, 42, 44, 46, 48–49, 52, 55, 56–57, 61, 66–67, 70, 72, 74, 76–77, 81, 84, 86–87, 90, 93, 96, 100; Mark Duncan/AP Images, 6–7; Josh Reynolds/AP Images, 14–15; Library of Congress, 22; Corbis, 25; The Mariners' Museum/Corbis, 26–27; Universal Images Group/SuperStock, 29; US Coast Guard/AP Images, 62; Phil Sandlin/AP Images, 64; AlexanderZam/Thinkstock, 89

Editor: Arnold Ringstad
Series Designer: Jake Nordby

Library of Congress Control Number: 2014932874

Cataloging-in-Publication Data

Marciniak, Kristin.
 The US Coast Guard / Kristin Marciniak.
  p. cm. -- (Essential library of the US military)
 ISBN 978-1-62403-434-3
 1. United States. Coast Guard--Juvenile literature.   I. Title.
 363.28/60973--dc23

2014932874

CONTENTS

CHAPTER ONE

SURVIVING A SUPERSTORM

Hurricane winds howled as the tall, three-masted ship violently lurched back and forth amid two-story-tall waves. The ship's 16-person crew had spent the day securing every piece of furniture and equipment onboard. Now they held on to anything they could find. Walking across the slippery, rain-soaked main deck was

treacherous, but the churning ocean below was far more deadly. One wrong step or loosened grasp and you would be tossed from the ship like a rag doll.

Things were not any better belowdecks. Brutal waves pitched the 169-foot (52 m) ship back and forth, slamming the captain into a table and sending a crew member flying across the tween deck.[1] The captain severely injured his back; the crew member had three broken ribs.

The ship was taking a similar beating. More water streamed in between the boat's wooden planks than its pumps could push out. The ship's generators malfunctioned and shut down completely. Without power, all pumping stopped. Water filled the bilge, the area between the bottom of the boat and the floor of the lowest level. It seeped onto the engine room floor and began rising quickly. Soon, the lowest level of the ship was submerged, and the tween deck was well on its way to flooding. The surging waters chased the crew from the ship's interior out onto the deck. They slipped on their

HURRICANE SANDY

Hurricane Sandy began as a tropical depression on October 22, 2012. By October 24, it became a Category 1 hurricane with winds anywhere from 74 to 95 miles per hour (119 to 153 kmh).[2] While they are the least disastrous class of hurricanes, Category 1 storms can still be deadly. Sandy left 70 dead in the Caribbean before moving northward to the United States.[3]

Sandy grew in size and strength as it moved up the East Coast, at one point measuring more than 900 miles (1,600 km) across.[4] It came ashore in southern New Jersey on Monday, October 29, bringing staggering winds, powerful rain, and surging seas to the surrounding states. Though the bulk of Sandy's damage was focused in the Northeast, the effects of the storm could be felt as far away as Michigan and Wisconsin. More than 100 Americans died as a result of the storm. Thousands lost their homes, and 8 million people were without power. In all, Sandy caused as much as $20 billion in damage.[5]

By the time the rescuers reached the *Bounty*, the ship had nearly slipped beneath the waves.

orange survival suits as the ship tilted to a precarious 45-degree angle.

It was just before 4:00 a.m. on Monday, October 29, 2012. In the midst of Hurricane Sandy, one of the fiercest storms the United States had ever seen, the *Bounty* was sinking 90 miles (145 km) off the coast of North Carolina. It was time to abandon ship.

THE DARING RESCUE

The *Bounty* was a beautiful ship, a painstakingly detailed replica of the famous boat of the same name from the 1700s. Built in 1960 for use in movies, it starred alongside Marlon Brando in *Mutiny on the Bounty* and Johnny Depp in *Pirates of the Caribbean: Dead Man's Chest*. But the ship was not just a Hollywood prop. It was built following the same plans used by the builders of the original *Bounty*, with additional headroom in the tween deck for movie cameras. The three tall masts and billowing sails brought to mind swashbuckling sailors and a life of adventure on the high seas.

The coast guard helicopter team that arrived on the scene just before dawn encountered a very different version of the *Bounty*. Its three masts barely jutted out of the sea; the rest was completely submerged in the roiling waters below. Nearby, two octagonal life rafts covered with bright orange tarps bobbed furiously in the Atlantic. Thirteen out of the 16 crew members were huddled in the life rafts. The others, including the captain, were floating in the sea alone.

The first of the three was found less than a mile (1.6 km) from the sinking ship.[6] Wearing night vision goggles, helicopter copilot Lieutenant Jane Pena

EPIRB MARKS THE SPOT

The search and rescue team was able to find the crew of the *Bounty* thanks to a small device called an Emergency Position Indicating Radio Beacon (EPIRB). Carried onboard most vessels, it transmits a signal on an emergency frequency. Once activated, it alerts the coast guard to the location of a ship in distress.

Some EPIRBs are activated manually, while others are automatically activated by water. In the event of a sinking, a mechanism releases the EPIRB, allowing it to float up to the water's surface. An antenna and strobe light help rescuers pinpoint the location of the sunken vessel and any survivors. The *Bounty*'s EPIRB activated automatically when the ship sank.

spotted a flashing signal on the crew member's orange survival suit.

While pilot Lieutenant Commander Steve Cerveny and Pena focused on keeping the MH-60 Jayhawk steady in the raging storm, flight mechanic Petty Officer Third Class Mike Lufkin lowered rescue swimmer Petty Officer Second Class Randy Haba into the frothing waters 300 feet (91 m) below. As Haba made his way to the stranded survivor, Lufkin carefully let down the rescue litter, which looks like a large basket with orange buoys on its sides.

Haba fought his way through the crashing waves back to the rescue basket, keeping a protective arm lashed around the survivor's chest. Once the survivor was safely secured in the basket, Lufkin hoisted the basket to the

Survival suits carried aboard the *Bounty* helped keep survivors warm while they awaited rescue.

SWIM SIGNALS

Rescue swimmers wear orange dive suits so they can be spotted easily from the air and sea, along with a harness that hooks onto a cable that pulls them up to the helicopter. A helmet with a radio headset allows the swimmer to keep in contact with the flight mechanic and pilots, but the noise of the ocean and the chopper make verbal communication nearly impossible. When in the water, the swimmer relies on hand signals to communicate with the team above.

helicopter. Moments later, Haba attached the chopper's cable to his harness and zipped up to join the rest of his team.

Their next stop was the first life raft, which had seven crew members aboard. Haba helped four more of them to safety. The helicopter was running out of fuel, so the backup chopper would have to get the rest of the survivors. After an hour fighting against the superstorm, Haba and the rest of the team escorted the first five survivors back to solid ground.

The second Jayhawk helicopter, piloted by Lieutenant Commander Steve Bonn and copilot Jenny Fields, soon arrived. Flight mechanic Petty Officer First Class Gregory Moulder ensured rescue swimmer Petty Officer Third Class Dan Todd made it safely to the second life raft. "Hi, I'm Dan," Todd said to the six survivors nervously huddled in the second raft. "I heard you guys need a ride."[7]

As Todd hauled the survivors to the rescue basket one by one, Bonn and Fields fought against Sandy's relentless winds from the cockpit. It was important the chopper stay steady while Moulder used the winch to reel in the rescue basket. In the background, the safety system that measures the distance between the bottom of the helicopter and the surface of the water was blaring out warnings. The pilot and copilot noticed the alarm but did not panic, instead focusing on the lives in their hands.

TWO LIVES LOST

More aircraft were sent to look for the two remaining *Bounty* sailors. Crew member Claudene Christian was found unresponsive several miles from the ship's original position. She died that night in the hospital. After 90 hours, the search for Captain Robin Walbridge was suspended. Both the coast guard and his family assume he went down with the ship.

All six people in the second life raft made it aboard the backup chopper, as did the remaining three from the first life raft, thanks to the team's tireless efforts. As Hurricane Sandy descended upon the eastern seaboard, the second Jayhawk headed back to the safety of the coast guard air station in Elizabeth City, North Carolina, where the survivors would be reunited with their loved ones.

The heroic rescue of the *Bounty* survivors will be told for decades to come, but for the coast guard teams in the line of duty, it was just another day at the office. "It was good that we got to go help people," said rescue swimmer Todd. "We were just doing the job."[8]

CHAPTER TWO
ORIGINS

The coast guard is the oldest maritime service in the United States. As one of the five branches of the US military, its members have served in every US war with the exception of the Korean War (1950–1953). The US Coast Guard we know today actually began as five separate federal agencies: the Lighthouse Service, the Revenue

Cutter Service, the Lifesaving Service, the Steamboat Inspection Service, and the Bureau of Navigation. Each service operated independently but shared similar duties and authorities. They also shared the same basic purpose: protecting people and saving lives.

THE LIGHTHOUSE SERVICE

The Lighthouses Act of 1789 was one of the first laws passed by the fledgling US government. Its purpose was to encourage commerce via the Atlantic Ocean by providing safe passage for ships carrying goods. In an age without radios and the global positioning system (GPS), lighthouses were extremely important in letting ships know the coast was near. Without them, ships could easily end up hitting a rocky shore in the middle of dark, stormy nights. Until the act was passed, all lighthouses were built and run by the individual states. Under the new law, existing lighthouses became the property of the federal government, and money for new lighthouses, beacons, and buoys came from federal taxes. The Department of the Treasury oversaw lighthouses.

More than 1,000 lighthouses were built over the next century.[1] Each lighthouse was run by a keeper whose

IDA LEWIS, LIGHTHOUSE LIFESAVER

In the 1800s, the government employed 400 women as keepers of lighthouses. At the time, women could typically only find employment as clerks, maids, field hands, teachers, and factory workers. Many female lighthouse workers came into their positions after the death of a husband or father who was serving as keeper. That is how Ida Lewis earned her position as lightkeeper and rescuer.

While tending a lighthouse with her father at age 15, Lewis rescued four men whose boat had capsized off the coast of Newport, Rhode Island. After her father passed away, Lewis assumed the role of keeper. She single-handedly rescued up to 25 people during her tenure in the lighthouse. When Lewis died in 1911, all the boats in the harbor tolled their bells in her honor.

appointment was approved by the president of the United States. It was a lonely job, with just one keeper appointed per lighthouse, and it did not pay well. Many keepers had to take additional jobs just to support their families. Some keepers hired assistants to keep the lights burning while they were away from the lighthouse; others recruited their wives and children to help.

A lighthouse keeper's task was simple: light the oil lamp every evening at sunset and ensure it burned until sunrise. While this seems like an easy enough job, it was not unusual for a lamp to burn out by 3:00 or 4:00 a.m. A dark lighthouse meant trouble for ships at sea, so the keeper had to be vigilant about keeping the lamp lit.

The US Department of Labor and Commerce took over responsibility for lighthouses in 1903. Ten years later, the department was split into the Department of Labor and the Department of Commerce. Lighthouses were overseen by the Department of Commerce. Lighthouses remained one of the main sources for maritime navigation up until the 1990s. Most modern ships use GPS for navigation, making lighthouses all but obsolete. The coast guard still takes care of short-range navigation aids, such as buoys and markers, but nearly all lighthouses have been decommissioned. The lone remaining coast guard lighthouse is in Boston Harbor.

REVENUE CUTTER SERVICE

Founded in 1790 as the Revenue Marine Service, the Revenue Cutter Service was the blueprint for today's US Coast Guard. Its responsibilities, duties, and ethos are so closely aligned with what we have come to expect from the modern US Coast Guard that most government officials cite 1790 as the branch's birth date.

Alexander Hamilton, the first secretary of the Treasury, came up with the idea for the Revenue Cutter Service in 1789. The Department of the Treasury would oversee this agency. The newly independent United States did not have much income, relying on import taxes for 90 percent of all federal revenues.[2] After years of smuggling goods into the colonies to avoid British fees, colonists were now expected to pay taxes on everything that came into port. Enforcement was

STOPPING THE SLAVE TRADE

The Revenue Cutter Service enforced more than just tax laws at sea. The number of slaves transported from Africa greatly increased after the invention of the cotton gin in 1793. The device made it easier to produce cotton fibers, making slavery more lucrative for slave owners. Navy vessels were prohibited from participating in the slave trade in 1794, and by 1808 all slave imports were banned in the United States. The Revenue Cutter Service was tasked with seizing slave ships and releasing the captives. Unfortunately, the owners and crews of the ships were hardly ever convicted of their crimes, and the slave trade continued to operate illegally. Still, the Revenue Cutter Service managed to free at least 500 slaves before the start of the Civil War (1861–1865).[3]

At a 2012 event, coast guardsmen wore historic uniforms to commemorate the Revenue Cutter Service.

difficult. Hamilton proposed ten cutters be stationed on the Atlantic coast to uphold tax laws.

The Continental navy disbanded in 1790 following the Revolutionary War (1775–1781). The Revenue Cutter Service was the only seagoing military force in the United States until the establishment of the US Navy in 1798. Since the Revenue Cutter Service eventually became the US Coast Guard, the branch is officially the oldest continuous seagoing service in the United States. The Revenue Cutter Service was not a formidable military force; only 100 men crewed those first ten ships.[4] The nation's coast was thinly populated, and visits from commercial ships were not frequent. But as the country expanded, so did the number of cutters and their responsibilities.

Those responsibilities eventually grew to include suppressing piracy, protecting the country's timber reserves, and regulating navigation in US waters. The Revenue Cutter Service was also tasked with enforcing maritime safety requirements, such as having onboard lifesaving equipment, using adequate lighting at night, and possessing appropriate merchant ship documentation.

The Revenue Cutter Service also aided ships in distress. Lifesaving was not part of the service's explicit mission, but the men of the Revenue Cutter Service knew saving lives was part of the job. It became a formal requirement in the winter of 1831 when Secretary of the Treasury Louis McLane ordered the *Gallatin* to look for sailors in distress. This was the first time a US government agency was specifically ordered to patrol for people in danger, but it would not be the last.

UNITED STATES LIFESAVING SERVICE

The US Lifesaving Service was officially formed in 1878, but its beginnings date back to 1848, when the US government built lifesaving stations up and down the East Coast. The stations, mostly glorified sheds, were stocked with flares, ropes, and lanterns. But while the government had provided equipment and facilities, they had not provided employees. Instead, authorities selected trustworthy individuals from nearby towns and handed them the keys to the equipment shed and a printed set of instructions. Volunteers were rounded up in the event of an emergency, but few had any official lifesaving training. Equipment was not maintained or regularly inspected.

In 1871, lifesaving became an official mission of the federal government, bringing an expanded budget and sweeping improvements. Officers from the Revenue Cutter Service oversaw the reorganization of the lifesaving service, inspecting stations, purchasing new equipment, and training the crews.

The reorganization was not enough. In 1877 and 1878, two ships ran aground on sandbars. More than 180 men died waiting for help that never came. Spurred by public outrage, Congress officially authorized the

STRANDED CLOSE TO SHORE

Navigation in the 1800s and early 1900s relied on lighthouses, lightships, and buoys. While helpful, they were not foolproof. It was not uncommon for a ship to become stranded in shallow water or atop a sandbar. This was especially true during a storm when it was hard to see.

A grounded ship did not stand a chance against a raging storm. Even the sturdiest wooden ships could be blown to pieces within just a few hours. Until the Lifesaving Service was established, the thinly populated coastal areas offered little in the way of help for the stranded sailors. The only option was attempting to swim to shore through cold, rough waters. Those who managed to survive the waves often died of exposure to the elements once they reached shore.

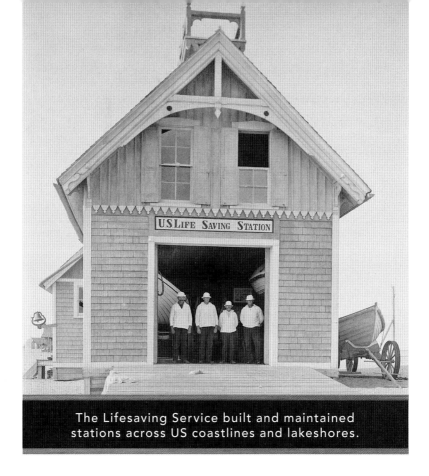

The Lifesaving Service built and maintained stations across US coastlines and lakeshores.

establishment of the US Lifesaving Service as an agency within the Treasury Department in 1878.

Under the direction of Sumner Kimball, the chief of the Treasury Department's Revenue Marine Division, the Lifesaving Service became a regimented operation with high performance standards. Six men plus a keeper were assigned to each station, and they spent their days and nights preparing for maritime disasters. Beaches were continuously patrolled, lookouts were established, and endless hours were spent practicing in lifeboats and smaller surfboats. Now, when a ship ran aground on a sandbar or suffered a catastrophic fire, the well-prepared station crew immediately sprang into action. The surfmen, named for the way they launched their boats from open beaches into the surf, braved raging seas to rescue mariners in distress.

STEAMBOAT INSPECTION SERVICE AND BUREAU OF NAVIGATION

Lifesaving services were not just necessary on the Atlantic coast. Inland waterways, such as the Great Lakes and the Mississippi River, had plenty of boating traffic. In the 1800s, most river and lake traffic consisted of merchant vessels delivering goods, but some vessels, such as

LIFESAVING SERVICE STATIONS

The Lifesaving Service operated three types of stations on the East Coast and along the Great Lakes. The first type, lifesaving stations, at first employed full-time crews only from November through April. This was the time in which most shipwrecks were likely to occur. By the beginning of the 1900s, most lifesaving stations operated year-round. Workers launched lightweight boats straight from the beach.

The second type, lifeboat stations, were located in or near port cities, mostly surrounding the Great Lakes. Here, lifeboats could be launched directly into deep water from a pier or ramp. The third type, houses of refuge, were found in South Carolina, Georgia, and Florida. These stations did not have active rescue crews. Instead, each one relied on one keeper and a small boat. The warmer climate meant shipwrecked sailors would not die quickly from exposure.

steamboats, also carried passengers. The steamboat was relatively new in the early 1800s, and Congress avoided imposing regulations on the fledgling industry until 1838. In that year, new laws required owners of steam vessels to employ skilled engineers and provide safety equipment such as lifeboats, fire pumps, hoses, and signal lights. The 1838 laws also required annual hull inspections and semiannual boiler inspections.

Boilers were a problem. They had a tendency to explode, setting ships ablaze and forcing survivors overboard. Collisions with other vessels were also common, as were smaller fires. Congress once again tightened steamboat regulations with the Steamboat Act of May 30, 1852. This law, under the guidance of the Department of Treasury, was the beginning of a formal inspection service. It required licensing for all pilots and engineers of steamboats, as well as extensive boiler testing, but it did not apply to freight boats, ferries, tugboats, or towboats.

A new set of laws passed in 1871 resulted in the creation of the Steamboat Inspection Service. These laws applied to all steam vessels and were designed to protect both crews and passengers. The service was also given the authority to inspect steam vessels. If inspectors found serious issues, they had the power to take away the license of the boat's crew.

While the Steamboat Inspection Service took on the job of ensuring safety laws were followed, the Bureau of Navigation dealt with other aspects of boating law. Founded in 1884 as part of the Department of Commerce, the Bureau of Navigation enforced the laws dealing with the hiring and firing of sailors, as well as enforcing appropriate conduct. Essentially, the Bureau of Navigation handled everything the other four maritime agencies did not.

By 1885, the basic framework of maritime law in the United States was set up. A complicated web of agencies handled a wide range of duties. In the 1900s, this collection of authorities would slowly be unified, eventually becoming the US Coast Guard we know today.

Steamboats made travel on US rivers faster, but they also introduced new dangers that made oversight critical.

CHAPTER THREE
A NEW BEGINNING

By the early 1900s, it was widely understood the Revenue Cutter Service was a valuable component of the US government. But there had always been a question of where it really belonged. Some in Washington, DC, thought it should be under the umbrella of the navy. Others believed it should remain as a separate entity.

Professor Frederick A. Cleveland of the Commission
on Economy and Efficiency thought the Revenue Cutter
Service should not exist at all. In 1911, he recommended
the service be formally disbanded. He reasoned some of
the Revenue Cutter Service's missions, such as stopping
slave ships, were obsolete. The rest of its duties could be

taken on by other government branches, such as the navy. Cleveland also recommended a merger of the Lifesaving Service and the Lighthouse Service.

Naturally, the Cleveland Commission's recommendation was extremely unpopular with the leaders of the Revenue Cutter Service. It was also unpopular with the navy. Navy officials maintained that it would be impossible to take on the mission of the Revenue Cutter Service without interfering with the navy's own mission, training for war. Secretary of the Treasury Franklin MacVeagh agreed but offered his own solution, suggesting the Revenue Cutter Service merge with the Lifesaving Service. Despite some naysayers, in April 1912, President William Howard Taft forwarded to Congress the Cleveland Commission's recommendation to disband the Revenue Cutter Service.

SAVED BY DISASTER

Within ten days of the president sending the Cleveland Commission's report to Congress, two horrific maritime events occurred. The first was a fire on the *Ontario* near Long Island, New York. All passengers were saved thanks to teamwork from the Revenue Cutter Service and the Lifesaving Service.

The second disaster was the sinking of the *Titanic*. The *Titanic* was one of the largest ships ever built. Its maiden voyage from Southampton, England, to New York City was cut short when the ship hit an iceberg in North Atlantic waters on April 14, 1912. There were not enough lifeboats for all of the passengers and crew, so women and children were evacuated first. More than 1,500 of the ship's 2,224 passengers and crew perished as the magnificent ship sank to its watery grave.[1]

The resulting investigations changed maritime law, including the addition of a requirement that boats carry enough lifeboats for every passenger. But it also changed the fate of the Revenue Cutter Service. Immediately after the *Titanic* sank, the US Navy sent two ships to patrol northern waters. After two months, those duties were passed to the Revenue Cutter Service. The service had years of experience in the frozen seas of Alaska, and it

The sinking of the *Titanic* had a dramatic indirect effect on the future of the Revenue Cutter Service.

CHANGING AGENCIES

In 1915, the newly formed coast guard was assigned to the Department of the Treasury, a civilian agency. The Treasury is responsible for the economic and financial systems of the United States, including imports and exports. One of the coast guard's many responsibilities is to protect maritime shipping lanes, thereby also protecting international trade. The Department of the Treasury seemed to be the best fit for the new agency.

In 1967, the coast guard was moved to the newly created Department of Transportation. The Department of Transportation took on responsibility for the safety of all transportation in the United States, including maritime transportation. The coast guard remained in the Department of Transportation for 36 years until the creation of the Department of Homeland Security in 2003.

knew how to handle ice floes drifting on the water's surface.

With this new mission, disbanding the Revenue Cutter Service was no longer an option. Now, Secretary of the Treasury MacVeagh's merger recommendation was passed on to Congress instead. On January 28, 1915, President Woodrow Wilson signed the documents combining the Revenue Cutter Service and the Lifesaving Service. The US Coast Guard was born.

A NEW ERA

The law President Wilson signed in 1915 named the US Coast Guard as a military force under the Department of Treasury during times of peace. During times of war, or at the president's discretion, it would be considered part of the navy, resuming its separate status at war's end. In 1939, the duties of the Lighthouse Service were folded into the coast guard's list of missions, giving the US Coast Guard full responsibility for lighthouses, buoys, and other navigational guides and markers.

The last two services of the original five, the Steamboat Inspection Service and the Bureau of

MARINES SALUTE
COAST GUARD
FOR THEIR BIG PART IN
THE INVASION OF
GUAM
"THEY PUT US HERE AND
WE INTEND TO STAY"

Navigation, were merged in 1936 as the Bureau of Marine Inspection and Navigation under the Department of Commerce and Labor. The new bureau's duties included enforcing laws dealing with the construction, safety, operation, equipment, inspection, and documentation of merchant vessels. The bureau was also responsible for investigating marine casualties, enforcing navigation laws, and licensing merchant vessel personnel. In 1942, President Franklin Roosevelt moved the Bureau of Marine Inspection and Navigation to the coast guard for the duration of World War II (1939–1945). The assignment became permanent in 1946, bringing all functions of maritime safety and law under the jurisdiction of one government agency. The formation of the modern US Coast Guard was complete.

THE COAST GUARD TODAY

Today, the US Coast Guard is both a military force and a law enforcement agency. Its missions support three primary maritime roles: safety, security, and stewardship. Every day, representatives of the coast guard protect the citizens, property, and resources of the United States from internal and external threats—both natural and man-made.

These threats are always changing, and the focus of the coast guard has changed along with them. In the late 1920s and the 1930s, the coast guard focused on intercepting contraband in accordance with Prohibition, the national ban on purchasing alcoholic beverages. The first half of the 1940s was dedicated to fighting World War II in Europe and the Pacific; civilian safety at sea and navigation became priorities when the conflict ended. Law enforcement was emphasized in the 1960s as Cuban refugees fled to the United States' southern shores, and contraband became a hot topic once again in the 1970s as drug runners attempted to smuggle narcotics through US waters.

The most recent shift in priorities happened after September 11, 2001, when the United States was victim to a devastating terrorist plot. The coast guard turned its

The modern US Coast Guard's focus on security is highlighted by its side-by-side harbor patrols with US Navy vessels.

focus to protecting US citizens and borders. In 2003, the coast guard moved from its home in the Department of Transportation to become the only military force in the newly created Department of Homeland Security.

Today, the men and women of the US Coast Guard are stationed on land, seas, rivers, and lakes. They protect 95,000 miles (153,000 km) of coastline and hundreds of ports.[2] They direct port traffic and provide waterway security. They respond to reports of water pollution, oil spills, and violation of marine wildlife protection laws. They fight on the front lines of the drug war and rescue people struggling at sea. They educate boaters and rescue those who have strayed too far from shore. The US Coast Guard is, as its motto states, *Semper Paratus*—Always Ready.

TOTAL FORCE

Active duty members make up just a part of the US Coast Guard. The branch also includes the US Coast Guard Reserve and the US Coast Guard Auxiliary. Both organizations assist the enlisted members of the US Coast Guard with fulfilling its missions as outlined by law.

The US Coast Guard Reserve was originally a civilian organization created in 1939 to help promote safety on the water, boatmanship, and knowledge of laws and regulations. In 1941, the reserve was split into two separate entities, the US Coast Guard Reserve and the US Coast Guard Auxiliary. Today, auxiliary volunteers educate the public about water and boating safety and also perform inspections of recreational vessels. The reserve, on the other hand, is a source of additional manpower during wartime. Its stated mission is to "support the Coast Guard roles of maritime homeland security, national defense (domestic and expeditionary), and domestic disaster operations."[3]

COAST GUARD BUDGET

ESTIMATED BUDGET
FISCAL YEAR 2014

Operating Expenses	$6,755,383,000
Environmental Compliance and Restoration	$13,187,000
Reserve Training	$109,543,000
Acquisition, Construction, and Improvements	$951,116,000
Research, Development, Test, and Evaluation	$19,856,000
Health-Care Fund Contribution	$186,602,000
Retired Pay	$1,452,150,000
Boating Safety	$109,464,000
Maritime Oil Spill Program	$238,600,000
Gift Fund	$80,000
Oil Spill Liability Trust Fund	-$45,000,000
Unspent Funds from Previous Budgets	-$42,000,000
Total Budget	$9,793,981,000[4]

ARMED SERVICES BUDGET
FISCAL YEAR 2014

Army	$129,700,000,000
Navy/Marines	$155,800,000,000
Air Force	$144,400,000,000[5]
Coast Guard	$9,793,981,000[6]

CHAPTER FOUR

A FORMIDABLE FLEET

The diversity of the coast guard's missions requires a versatile fleet of cutters, boats, airplanes, and helicopters, as well as specialized equipment for land and sea rescue operations. Whether they're delivering supplies to the Arctic, chasing drug traffickers, or rescuing

hurricane victims, the coast guard prides itself on having the right tools for the job.

Originally, the term *cutter* referred to any single-masted, gaff-rigged vessel with at least two sails set ahead of the mast. Cutters were the vessel of choice for the Revenue Cutter Service, and over time the name became

RACING STRIPES

Whether it is at sea, on land, or in the air, you can always identify a coast guard vessel by the orange and blue slash boldly painted along its side. Initially suggested by President John F. Kennedy in the early 1960s as a way to make coast guard vehicles more recognizable, the racing stripe was adopted service-wide in 1967. Maritime law enforcement agencies and safety organizations all over the world have adopted this distinctive design as a symbol of safety at sea.

synonymous with any vessel deployed for protecting the coasts.

Today, the coast guard classifies any ship longer than 65 feet (20 m) as a cutter. Cutters stay at sea for long periods of time, so there are living quarters for the crew. They usually carry a motor surfboat and a rigid-hull inflatable boat to use for smaller missions.

The coast guard's most powerful cutters are its icebreakers. Twin cutters *Polar Sea* and *Polar Star*, built in the 1970s, are 399 feet (122 m) long; the *Healy*, built in 2000, is 420 feet (128 m) long.[1] The *Healy* is named for Captain Michael Healy, who led the efforts of the Revenue Cutter Service in Alaskan waters in the late 1800s. All three icebreakers serve in the Arctic and Antarctic, delivering supplies to remote stations, operating search and rescue missions, and monitoring mining and drilling operations. They're also home to scientists studying the Arctic and Antarctic.

These icebreakers live up to their name. *Healy* can continuously break ice 4.5 feet (1.4 m) thick at a speed of

3.5 miles per hour (5.6 kmh).[2] *Polar Sea* and *Polar Star* can break through 6 feet (1.8 m) of ice at the same speed.[3] At slower speeds, *Polar Sea* and *Polar Star* can break through ice up to 21 feet (6.4 m) thick.[4] Their curved, reinforced hulls allow them to ride up on the ice and then break it with their weight. This feature sets them apart from the rest of the coast guard's cutter fleet.

The National Security Cutter is the newest and largest class of coast guard cutter used in the continental United States. These 418-foot- (127 m) long ships were constructed with homeland security in mind. Each cutter has several weapons systems that can stop rogue vessels far from shore, as well as systems for detection of and defense against missile attacks. A large flight deck allows helicopters to land and take off. The vessel and its crew of 122 patrol for 60 or 90 days at a time, engaging in a variety of jobs, including fishery patrols, sea rescues, homeland security patrols, disaster relief, and stopping illegal immigrants and drug smugglers.[5] These same duties are undertaken by the crews of the 270-foot (82 m) and 210-foot (64 m) medium endurance cutters, which stay at sea for shorter periods of time.

Buoy tenders also fall within the cutter category. The 225-foot (69 m) Seagoing Buoy Tenders and 175-foot (53 m) Coastal Buoy Tenders have excellent maneuverability, which makes them perfect for tending

THE NATIONAL SECURITY CUTTER

Helipad

Phalanx CIWS

57 mm Bofors gun

Nulka decoys

RHIB

U.S. COAST GUARD

751

Helipad: The cutter's helipad provides a place for helicopters to land and take off.

Phalanx CIWS: The Phalanx close-in weapon system, a six-barreled 20 mm machine gun, automatically detects and fires on missiles and aircraft that approach the ship.

57 mm Bofors gun: This light naval gun fires explosive ammunition.

RHIB: Rigid-hull inflatable boats let coast guard personnel approach and board ships.

Nulka decoys: Nulka decoys fire rockets that hover in the air and emit powerful radar signals to distract incoming anti-ship missiles, sending them flying away from the ship.

to buoys and other navigational aids offshore and in restricted waters. Large buoy tenders employ GPS to keep the ship steady in high winds, allowing the crew to service and accurately position buoys. Smaller vessels, such as the 65- and 75-foot (20 and 23 m) River Buoy Tenders, help position similar buoys in rivers and other inland bodies of water.

BOATS

Any coast guard vessel less than 65 feet (20 m) long is classified as a boat rather than a cutter. Boats usually operate near shore or in inland waterways. The coast guard's new shoreline emergency communication system, Rescue 21, can help rapidly and accurately transmit requests for assistance from ships in trouble.

The 45-foot (14 m) Response Boat-Medium (RB-M) is one of the coast guard's most versatile boats. The RB-M, which holds a crew of four, is used for many different tasks. It sees use in

RESCUE 21

The coast guard's advanced communications system is known as Rescue 21. Under development since 2003, it replaces the outdated National Distress and Response System. The new system can more accurately identify a distressed caller's location. It covers at least 23 miles (37 km) away from the shore, making it a key lifesaving tool for boaters in peril.[6]

The coast guard completed the installation of Rescue 21 sites along US coasts halfway through 2012. The system covers 42,000 miles (68,000 km) of coastline along the Great Lakes, the Atlantic and Pacific coasts, as well as Hawaii, Puerto Rico, Guam, the US Virgin Islands, and the Northern Mariana Islands.[7] Expansion to Alaska and rivers in the interior, including the Mississippi and Ohio River valleys, began in 2013.

Two small response boats escort a ferry
in New York City in April 2009.

search and rescue operations, stopping smugglers, and
providing security in ports. With its light, all-aluminum
frame, RB-Ms can hit speeds higher than 46 miles per
hour (74 kmh).[8] They have a sophisticated navigation
system, a communications system connected to federal,
state, and local homeland security organizations, and
weapon mounts.

The Response Boat-Small was developed in response
to the events of September 11, 2001. These 25-foot (8 m)

boats can operate with only two crew members and handle rough seas at high speeds. The US Coast Guard's Maritime Safety and Security Teams, Maritime Security Response Team, and Maritime Safety Units and Boat Stations all use these boats, as do other Department of Homeland Security agencies.

Search and rescue teams rely on the 47-foot (14 m) motor lifeboat, which is used for rescues in high seas, surf, and bad weather. Built to withstand the toughest sea conditions, the boats are self-bailing, self-righting, and nearly unsinkable. If a motor lifeboat does capsize, it is designed to right itself within seconds.

The coast guard also employs specialty vessels, including the 33-foot (10 m) Law Enforcement Special Purpose Craft, which is used for high-speed pursuits. Airboats up to 24 feet (7 m) long are used for ice rescue

FIREPOWER

Historically, the coast guard has not been known for its weaponry, but the shift to homeland security has resulted in more guns for the branch.

Like many other Department of Homeland Security agencies, coast guardsmen involved in law enforcement duties carry the compact Sig Sauer P229 pistol. It weighs less than two pounds (0.9 kg) when loaded and holds between 10 and 13 rounds.[9] Other coast guardsmen use the M16A2 rifle. The rifle can hit targets hundreds of feet away.

The entire coast guard helicopter fleet carries M-240 machine guns. These deadly accurate weapons have their bullets fed in quickly on belts. They are used to fire warning shots across the bows of speeding boats during high-speed ocean pursuits. Coast guard gunners will sometimes aim at the engine block to disable a boat. Most boaters are smart enough to stop.

missions and flood response. They can operate on top of water and ice, and they even travel short distances on land.

AIRCRAFT

The coast guard may be a maritime agency, but its members spend a lot of time in the sky. Airplanes and helicopters are both used for surveillance, security, and search and rescue.

The newest addition to the aircraft fleet is the HC-144A Ocean Sentry airplane. The Ocean Sentry is mostly used for patrol, but it also does medium-range surveillance. It has a wingspan of almost 85 feet (26 m) and a maximum speed of 283 miles per hour (455 kmh).[10]

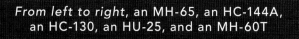

From left to right, an MH-65, an HC-144A, an HC-130, an HU-25, and an MH-60T

U.S. COAST GUARD

The Ocean Sentry replaced the HU-25, which performed a similar role, in 2014.

The HC-130 Hercules has undergone several reinventions since the coast guard first began using it in 1958. Today's airplane has a wingspan of 133 feet (41 m) and a cruising speed of 374 miles per hour (602 kmh). It can hold up to 92 passengers. It can also haul up to 51,000 pounds (23,000 kg) of cargo, rescue gear, or other equipment. The crew of seven can airdrop life rafts or even chemicals to break up oil slicks.[11]

Helicopters have been used in the coast guard since the end of World War II, when the service realized they could be used for search and rescue missions. Since then, helicopters have become a staple of the coast guard's aviation fleet.

The MH-65 Dolphin is the primary coast guard helicopter aboard certified cutters, such as the National Security Cutters. The Dolphin is designed to fly well at night and in all weather conditions except ice storms. Its rotors span 39 feet (12 m) and it cruises at 170 miles per hour (274 kmh). There are approximately 100 Dolphins in the coast guard fleet. Each is crewed by four guardsmen: two pilots, one mechanic, and one rescue swimmer.[12]

The MH-60T Jayhawk is a variation of the US Army's H-60 Blackhawk helicopter. Specialized for search and rescue missions, it is also operated by a crew of four and

Jayhawk crews train closely with guardsmen
on boats to ensure safe operations.

can fly in all weather. In addition to an advanced navigation system, it carries all of the equipment needed for a sea rescue. Larger than the Dolphin, the Jayhawk's rotors are 54 feet (16 m) in diameter, and it has a maximum speed of 207 miles per hour (333 kmh).[13]

The coast guard's many diverse missions call for a wide variety of watercraft and aircraft. Its assortment of ships of many shapes and sizes ensures the coast guard will always have the equipment it needs to carry out its job.

UPDATING THE FLEET

In the late 1990s, the coast guard determined that much of its existing fleet would soon simultaneously reach retirement age. Outdated vessels and aircraft are expensive to maintain. The branch decided to begin replacing them with modern vessels. The replacement process is scheduled to take at least 25 years. Between 2002 and 2006, civilian companies managed the project. In 2007, the coast guard reclaimed leadership of the project and renamed it Acquisition Directorate.

The National Security Cutters, the RB-Ms, and the Ocean Sentry are all results of this $30 billion initiative, as are updates to existing Jayhawk and Dolphin helicopters.[14] These new vessels and aircraft have up-to-date navigation and sensor capabilities and were designed with the coast guard's new focus on homeland security in mind.

CHAPTER FIVE
MARITIME SAFETY

A t its most basic level, a nation's primary responsibility is to ensure the safety of its citizens. The US armed services ensure safety overseas. Within the United States, state and local police handle this. The coast guard also operates on US soil and waterways. Most homeland maritime duties are handled by the coast guard. Two coast

Safety inspections of all kinds of vessels are a key part of the US Coast Guard's mission.

guard missions fall under this category: marine safety and search and rescue.

The US Coast Guard has learned a lot in its nearly 225 years of existence. The boiler explosions of steamboats in the 1800s and ocean liner disasters of the early 1900s prompted the coast guard to make sweeping changes to maritime policy and practice. Today, prevention is key in keeping people safe on the water. In addition to developing standards and regulations for commercial and recreational vessels, the coast guard inspects all types of watercraft.

Commercial inspections begin before construction even starts. Coast guard naval architects review, revise, and approve blueprints for each proposed vessel that will fly the US flag. When construction is complete, coast guard inspectors crawl through every nook and cranny of the ship to make sure all applicable laws are followed. Every aspect of each domestic commercial vessel is documented before it goes to sea, including its size, weight, and capacity. The men and women who crew these commercial vessels are also educated and licensed by the coast guard.

As the coordinator of boating safety, the coast guard treats the safety of recreational boaters with just as much

EARLY LIFESAVING EQUIPMENT

Search and rescue equipment has come a long way since the days of the Lifesaving Service. Early crews used a device called a Lyle gun to throw a line from the shore to a ship in distress. It resembled a cannon and could fire a line several hundred feet away.

Once the line was securely fastened, the men on shore readied the life car. Life cars were small metal boats with a sealable hatch, like a submarine.

Connected to the line, life cars could haul up to 11 people back to shore. They were heavy and hard to handle.

An easier way to transfer people along the line was with a breeches buoy. It resembled a donut-shaped life preserver with a pair of canvas pants attached. Pulleys sent it out to the ship in distress. After the sailor stepped into the pants, he was pulled back to shore.

care as the safety of commercial boaters. In this position, the coast guard works hard to minimize loss of life and personal injury in boating accidents. It also strives to prevent damage to the environment by civilian boaters.

The US Coast Guard Auxiliary works to educate recreational boaters. It also inspects boats and oversees the boat licensing process. Its 30,000 volunteers conduct vessel safety checks and teach classes to educate the general public about boating safety.[1]

When an accident does happen, the coast guard is immediately on the scene. Once all survivors are accounted for and safely back on land, coast guardsmen turn their focus to the causes of the accident. Maritime accidents are thoroughly investigated to determine whether laws were violated and if improvements should be made to the coast guard's prevention programs.

INTERNATIONAL MARITIME ORGANIZATION

The coast guard represents the United States in the International Maritime Organization (IMO), an arm of the United Nations. With a membership of 170 nations, the organization focuses on commercial ship safety at sea, pollution prevention, and mariner training. Representatives from each member nation work together to develop and enforce vessel construction standards as well as shipping and navigation regulations in an effort to fulfill the IMO's mission statement: "Safe, secure, and efficient shipping on clean oceans."[2]

SEARCH AND RESCUE

The coast guard strives to minimize the risks associated with maritime trade, travel, and recreation, but there will always be a need for search and rescue (SAR) teams to help mariners in distress. In 2012, the coast guard responded to 19,790 search and rescue cases, saving 3,560 lives and more than $77 million in property.[3] That is almost ten lives saved every day.

Some cases, such as the rescue of the *Bounty* survivors, are spectacular stories suited for the front pages of newspapers. But the majority of rescues occur when a well-meaning boater goes too far out to sea or misjudges the weather. In these cases, the coast guard might simply help guide the boat back to shore.

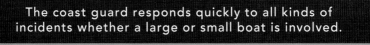

The coast guard responds quickly to all kinds of incidents whether a large or small boat is involved.

Some SAR teams use helicopters to aid mariners in more deadly situations. The helicopter's mechanic lowers a rescue swimmer wearing a harness attached to a retractable cable. A rescue basket or rescue litter follows, and the swimmer quickly secures the survivor into place. The mechanic raises the survivor into the helicopter then brings the rescue swimmer back up. The next survivor is located and the process begins all over again until the last person is safely out of the water.

Coast guard air crewmen and rescue swimmers are trained in first aid in case of a serious injury. These skills come in handy when transferring critically ill passengers to shore for immediate medical attention.

SAR GEAR

SAR teams use specialized equipment and gear to help pull people out of the water, save them from sinking ships, and get them safely back to shore. Rescue baskets, like the ones used during the rescue of the *Bounty*, hoist survivors from land or sea. Injured victims may be strapped onto a rescue litter, a stainless steel stretcher with flotation logs attached to its sides and chest pads. The foot of the litter is heavier than the head. During a water rescue, the foot end of the litter is in the water, which keeps the victim's head above water.

Rescue swimmers wear dry suits when entering water colder than 55 degrees Fahrenheit (13°C) and wet suits in warmer water.[4] Dry suits are tightly sealed to prevent cold water from touching the skin, while wet suits are looser. Every rescue swimmer also wears a rescue harness, which is a combination of a flotation device and a lift harness. When the harness is connected to a cable on the helicopter, the flight mechanic can raise and lower the rescue swimmer.

HURRICANE KATRINA

The largest coast guard rescue effort to date was in late August 2005 following the devastating effects of Hurricane Katrina. A tropical storm over the Bahamas turned into a Category 1 hurricane as it made landfall on eastern Florida, eventually becoming a Category 5 hurricane before it plowed into the Gulf Coast. Louisiana, Mississippi, and parts of Alabama and Florida were struck by the storm. New Orleans, Louisiana, was hit especially hard. More than 50,000 people were trapped in the city's residential areas, which flooded with more than 20 feet (6 m) of water.[5]

The coast guard was prepared. As the storm neared land, coast guardsmen from around the country gathered at the Aviation Training Center in Mobile, Alabama, temporarily creating the largest Coast Guard Air Station in history. When the worst of the storm was over, more than 40 coast guard aircraft took to the air, rescuing survivors from rooftops and attic windows. Pilots wore night vision goggles to continue rescues after the sun set, and the skies were filled with the whir of rotors signaling that help was on the way.

A total of 12,535 people were rescued by helicopter after Hurricane Katrina, and even more were shuttled to safety by small coast guard boats.[6] In all, more than 5,600 coast guardsmen saved 33,500 people in the first

Helicopters gave US Coast Guard pilots and crew members sobering views of Katrina's destruction.

few days after Katrina came ashore in New Orleans.[7] It was a monumental rescue effort accomplished in the worst circumstances: no electricity, no drinkable water, no food, no medical supplies, and no reliable communications. It was a defining moment for the US Coast Guard.

CHAPTER SIX

MARITIME SECURITY

While the coast guard gets significant recognition for its search and rescue efforts, the agency actually spends far more time engaging in law enforcement activities. The events of September 11, 2001, and the resulting creation of the Department of Homeland Security have served to

emphasize this role. Four coast guard missions fall under the umbrella of maritime security: defense readiness, drug interdiction, migrant interdiction, and ports, waterways, and coastal security.

DEFENSE READINESS

The coast guard has been part of nearly every major war since the establishment of the Revenue Cutter Service in 1790, generally serving under the navy during wartime. Historically, coast guardsmen serving overseas have helped with coastal patrols, established navigation aids, provided security forces, and rescued downed pilots and victims of ship or submarine disasters. As recently as 2012, the coast guard had a presence in Iraq, protecting Iraqi maritime oil infrastructure and training Iraqi naval forces.

In 2008, the Departments of Defense and Homeland Security formally outlined the coast guard's responsibilities in support of national military, defense, and security strategies. In times of peace, crisis, and war, the coast guard's responsibilities include intercepting watercraft on the sea and in the air, keeping people safe in the midst of environmental disasters such as oil spills, and protecting ports. But not every struggle is fought on foreign soil.

COAST GUARDSMEN IN WORLD WAR II

During World War II, the US Coast Guard coordinated landing operations for the US Army and US Marines in every important invasion in North Africa, Italy, France, and the Pacific. Coast guardsmen patrolled for enemy submarines and rescued survivors of torpedo attacks off the coast of the United States. Following enemy attacks on naval vessels, coast guard cutters saved soldiers from certain death aboard burning and sinking ships.

Some battles, such as the ongoing War on Drugs, take place at home.

DRUG INTERDICTION

In the 1920s and 1930s, the coast guard was tasked with enforcing Prohibition, the banning of the sale and transport of alcohol. By the late 1970s, the coast guard had prioritized the interception of illegally imported drugs. Cocaine was its biggest challenge. The drug can be easily concealed on cargo boats, and the potential payoff for the smugglers is very high. The savviest smugglers switched from rusty old freighters to sleek motorboats known as go-fasts.

Go-fasts were a problem. Coast guard ships were not able to keep up with the smugglers' high-performance speedboats. By 1998, the service was stopping less than

PROHIBITION

Between 1920 and 1933, a priority for the coast guard was the enforcement of the 18th Amendment to the Constitution. The amendment forbade the sale, manufacture, and importation of alcohol.

The battle between smugglers and the authorities became known as the Rum War. It took place mostly at sea. Smugglers labeled alcohol from Canada for shipment to Mexico or the Caribbean, but would instead divert the delivery to the United States. Coast guard cutters were stationed at sea to keep the contraband from reaching shore.

The smugglers' boats were faster than coast guard vessels, and the shootouts between smugglers and coast guardsmen resulted in loss of life on both sides. It took at least a decade for the coast guard's equipment to catch up with that of the smugglers, and by that time, Prohibition was on its way out. The amendment was repealed in 1933.

USE OF FORCE

The coast guard is in the unique position of being the only US armed service allowed to carry out domestic law enforcement duties. For example, if a riot broke out after a natural disaster and US Army helicopters were sent to control the scene, they would be unable to use any sort of force to subdue rioters unless martial law had been declared. The coast guard, on the other hand, is authorized to use force to enforce American laws, such as migrant and drug interdiction.

This is due to a law called the Posse Comitatus Act of 1878, which draws a clear line between military and domestic police forces. The act prohibits the use of the US Army, Navy, Marines, and Air Force for any law enforcement on US soil. The act does not apply to the coast guard, which is tasked with the bulk of maritime law enforcement duties.

10 percent of drugs entering the United States.[1] That same year, coast guard volunteers formed the Helicopter Interdiction Tactical Squadron (HITRON), which used helicopters to chase down speeding go-fasts. Within the team's first seven months, it stopped all five go-fasts it encountered, seizing $100 million worth of cocaine and marijuana.[2] With this success, the coast guard established more HITRON teams.

Based out of Jacksonville, Florida, HITRON teams and their helicopters are stationed aboard coast guard cutters for deployments of 30 to 60 days. During that time, the HITRON team works with a team in a maritime patrol aircraft, such as the Hercules, and a pursuit boat team on the cutter. When the Hercules spots a go-fast, the HITRON crew launches from the cutter to confirm whether the vessel is likely to be smuggling.

A HITRON team fires warning shots in a simulated mission against an empty go-fast.

The HITRON pilots use sirens, loudspeakers, and radio to tell the crew of the go-fast to stop. Then a team from the cutter boards the boat and searches for contraband.

If the go-fast does not stop, the helicopter team fires warning shots across the bow of the boat, then aims at the boat's engines if necessary. Once the boat is stopped, the coast guard boarding team embarks the go-fast and takes the smugglers into custody.

MIGRANT INTERDICTION

Smuggling is not limited to illegal narcotics. Every day, undocumented migrants risk life and limb during perilous journeys to the United States in hopes of finding safer, better homes than the ones they left behind.

The United States has strict immigration policies, including a limit on the number of permanent immigrants allowed into the country each year. There is a separate limit for refugees. Those who choose to bypass the formal immigration process are known as illegal immigrants. Many arrive by boat and therefore enter into the jurisdiction of the coast guard.

On May 1, 1980, a single boat brought approximately 500 Cuban immigrants to the United States.

The coast guard's migrant interdiction mission is twofold. Guardsmen provide a layer of defense to deter, detect, and interdict undocumented migrants from illegally entering the United States. But they must also help preserve the safety of migrants while they are at sea or aboard coast guard vessels. In some cases, this means coast guardsmen deliver food and water to desperate, dehydrated migrants or provide medical attention before ordering the migrants to turn around and head back to their home country.

For most undocumented migrants, a glimpse of the orange and blue coast guard racing stripe means a one-way trip back home. But if you are Cuban and make it past the coast guard to dry land, you are allowed to stay. This policy was established in 1994 after the Cuban government opened the port of Mariel in 1980.

THE MARIEL BOATLIFT

The coast guard's largest peacetime operation in history took place in 1980 when the Cuban government authorized the departure of anyone who wanted to leave Cuba. Hundreds of small boats left the port of Mariel in Cuba for Florida's shores, many of them in less-than-seaworthy condition and carrying far too many passengers.

It was a surprise announcement. The coast guard scrambled to oversee the mass exodus, calling in 900 reserve coast guardsmen to help safely get the Cuban migrants to shore. As refugees, most were welcomed into the United States. The operation was a success. Between April 15 and October 31, 1980, more than 125,000 Cuban immigrants landed on Florida's southern shores. A total of 27 perished at sea.[3]

Most Cubans continue to sail to the United States in rustic vessels, but some opt to pay for a spot on a go-fast. Smugglers charge $10,000 per seat and overcrowd the small boats with up to 30 passengers.[4] This results in enormous profit for successful smugglers.

PORTS, WATERWAYS, AND COASTAL SECURITY

Ninety percent of the world's trade is transported on the water. International trade generates thousands of jobs each year in the United States. If a disaster such as a terrorist attack struck a port, the US economy could be severely damaged.

In February 2010, the coast guard detained suspected illegal immigrants intercepted aboard a boat off the coast of California.

To ensure the safety of US citizens, as well as the economy, the coast guard inspects vessels and people that arrive in US ports. In 2012, coast guardsmen screened 49,000 recreational vessels, 117,000 commercial vessels, and 29.5 million crew members and passengers.[5]

The coast guard's other port, waterway, and coastal security duties include patrolling waterways, inspecting port facilities, controlling the movements of vessels in port, and serving as a first responder in the event of a crisis. As with drug and migrant interdiction, the coast guard uses force against anyone or anything threatening the safety and security of US interests.

SEPTEMBER 11

The coast guard activated one of the largest waterborne evacuations in history on September 11, 2001, after terrorists crashed two airplanes into the World Trade Center towers. New York City coast guardsmen rushed to New York Harbor, where they commandeered boats in an effort to get civilians off the island of Manhattan. By the day's end, more than 500,000 people had been evacuated by boat; tens of thousands more walked across the Brooklyn Bridge.[6]

The coast guard also took action to prevent any potential attacks on US waterways. Ports and harbors across the country shut down one by one, beginning with New York Harbor just seven minutes after the second plane crash.

The coast guard boards fishing boats to enforce regulations protecting sea life.

BOREAS
GUARDIA

CHAPTER SEVEN
MARINE STEWARDSHIP

The coast guard protects more than the citizens and property of the United States. It is also responsible for the care of the lakes, rivers, and oceans that create our borders and transport our goods, as well as the plants and animals that make their homes in these waters. To fulfill this mission, the coast guard simultaneously plays the roles of educator, emergency responder, and law enforcer. Such diverse missions as responding to oil spills, enforcing fishing laws, helping ships navigate, and clearing shipping paths through Arctic ice all contribute to the US Coast Guard's task of marine stewardship.

ILLEGAL FISHING

Illegal fishing is sometimes carried out using drift nets, large curtains of mesh netting suspended in the water by a system of floats and weights. Fish swim right into the invisible netting, as do other sea creatures including sharks, sea turtles, and even sea birds.

In 2000, the coast guard cutter *Sherman* stopped a Korean-owned fishing ship off the coast of Alaska and found a nine-mile- (14 km) long drift net that had caught 700 salmon, eight sharks, 50 puffin, 12 albatross, and a porpoise.[3] With the exception of the salmon, all would have been illegally sold to the highest bidder.

LIVING MARINE RESOURCES

Fishing is big business in the United States. US waters support commercial and recreational fisheries worth more than $30 billion each year.[1] An industry that large requires regulation to ensure stocks of fish and other marine resources, including endangered species, are not overfished beyond the point of no return.

The coast guard serves as the primary agency for at-sea fisheries enforcement, helping protect marine resources to ensure the future of fisheries for years to come. The coast guard also enforces the US Exclusive Economic Zone (EEZ). It extends 230 miles (370 km) from US coasts, covering nearly 3.4 million square miles (8.8 million sq km) of ocean.[2] Only US vessels and companies are allowed to fish in this area. Coast guardsmen patrol the borders of this zone to make sure foreign fishers are not poaching from US waters.

The coast guard also enforces foreign and international fishing laws outside of the EEZ, such as the United Nations' 1992 ban on large-scale drift nets in international waters. In areas where international agreements permit them to do so, coast guard boarding teams inspect every inch of fishing vessels, from the equipment to the catch. Those that are in compliance are free to go; companies or even nations that break the rules run the risk of no longer being able to sell their products in the United States.

MARINE ENVIRONMENTAL PROTECTION

The coast guard also protects fish, sea mammals, and endangered species by protecting their habitats from oil spills, hazardous materials, and invasive plants and animals. This is done through education and prevention programs, law enforcement, and disaster recovery.

Oil continues to be one of the biggest problems facing marine habitats today. The coast guard has helped contain oil spills as far

PROTECTING RESOURCES

The coast guard has been actively involved in environmental protection for almost 200 years. In 1822, Congress put the Revenue Cutter Service in charge of protecting a timber reserve of Florida live oak trees. These trees were deemed to be a critical component to US security because Florida live oaks provided the best wood for building warships. The Revenue Cutter Service patrolled the reserve to make sure there was no unauthorized use of the valuable timber.

Coast guard pilots fly an HC-144A over the site of the *Deepwater Horizon* spill to evaluate the progress of the disaster response.

away as the Strait of Malacca in the Indian Ocean and the Strait of Magellan at the southern tip of South America. But no disaster has hit quite so close to home as the *Deepwater Horizon* spill in 2010.

On April 20, 2010, an oil drilling rig named *Deepwater Horizon* exploded in the Gulf of Mexico approximately 50 miles (80 km) off the coast of Louisiana. Eleven workers were killed in the explosion and resulting fire, and the coast guard initially responded to the scene as a search and rescue operation. It soon became clear that oil was being released from the underground oil well, and the coast guard shifted its focus from search and rescue to controlling the leak and preventing oil from washing ashore.

Oil streamed through the gulf for three months, surpassing 1989's *Exxon Valdez* disaster in Alaska as the worst oil spill in US waters. The coast guard, along with the Minerals Management Service, is the primary regulator of drilling activity in US waters. After the spill, it was the coast guard's duty to ensure the owner of the rig capped the flow of oil from under the ocean floor. The service also led efforts to clean up floating oil before it reached shore.

The coast guard's day-to-day involvement with *Deepwater Horizon* ended in the summer of 2013, but its battle against oil spills will not end anytime soon. Despite the protective measures and regulations in place

EXXON VALDEZ

Before the *Deepwater Horizon* oil spill, the largest oil disaster in the United States was the *Exxon Valdez* spill in March 1989. The enormous oil tanker ran aground in Alaska's Prince William Sound, releasing 11 million gallons (42 million L) of crude oil. More than 350 miles (560 km) of coastline were covered in oil, and the cleanup effort required 450 vessels, including four coast guard cutters and four buoy tenders.[4]

The *Exxon Valdez* affected environmental protection standards the way the sinking of the *Titanic* affected marine safety. The disastrous accident ultimately led to the passage of the Oil Pollution Act of 1990. The law increased oversight of oil-carrying vessels, giving the coast guard its largest law enforcement duty since Prohibition.

The coast guard's buoy tenders transport and place buoys in US waters to aid navigation.

to prevent spills in open water, there are still thousands of spills each year.

AIDS TO NAVIGATION

One way the coast guard tries to prevent these large-scale accidents is by providing navigational aids. These aids include buoys, lights, fog signals, lightships, radio beacons, and electronic navigation systems. The coast guard also offers tide and current information and provides technical assistance.

Navigational aids do not just protect the marine environment. They also serve to direct a maritime trade industry that generates millions of jobs for American workers. Approximately 4,000 coast guardsmen maintain more than 96,000 aids to navigation every year to facilitate waterway commerce.[5] It is the coast guard's duty to make US waters safe for commercial and military ships.

ICE OPERATIONS

Safe and navigable waterways are harder to come by in cold weather. The coast guard uses smaller cutters to keep shipping lanes open on otherwise frozen rivers and lakes throughout the winter months. But some areas of the globe have more severe weather to deal with and far thicker ice.

The coast guard is the lead federal agency for ensuring maritime safety and security in the Arctic and Antarctic. This role unofficially began after the sinking of the *Titanic* in 1912 and the creation of the International Ice Patrol in 1914. The navy originally helmed the patrol, but the coast guard took over after two months. Since the service began, no ship has been lost to ice.

These frosty, ice-filled waters are also used for maritime commerce, and there is no better way to break ice than with the coast guard's three heavy-duty icebreakers. The *Polar Star*, the *Polar Sea*, and the *Healy* resupply US Arctic and Antarctic stations, provide search and rescue services, engage in law enforcement and environmental protection, and support research studies of the National

Science Foundation. The *Healy* alone provides lab space for up to 50 scientists at a time.[6]

The coast guard also works closely with local government and tribal officials in Alaska to address concerns about increased commercial traffic in the area and determine how the coast guard can provide assistance

The *Healy*, *left*, can clear a path through thick Arctic ice for smaller, more fragile ships.

to indigenous peoples. In 2012, the coast guard visited dozens of Arctic communities and schools to teach both children and adults about water and ice safety. Coast guardsmen also provided medical, dental, and veterinary assistance in some of the communities.

Outreach programs like these are what being in the coast guard is all about: educating the public about safety practices while protecting people and property from danger.

PROTECTING THE NORTH

The Revenue Cutter Service's early work in Alaska was focused on the protection of fur seals that were being hunted to near-extinction in the late 1800s. The patrol cutter on duty, the *Rush*, was known and feared by poachers. The crew of the *Rush*, as well as other patrol crews, successfully protected many seals.

Training exercises can be realistic, exciting, and even dangerous experiences.

CHAPTER EIGHT
TRAINING

Serving in the coast guard is not like serving in the other branches of the armed forces. Instead of training for months, maybe even years, before entering high-pressure combat zones, coast guardsmen are involved in a low-level conflict 365 days per year. Once boot camp is over, new recruits are out in the field, practicing maritime law enforcement and participating in sea rescues.

The coast guard's size is both a good thing and a bad thing. Working in such a small force means the voice of an individual person is more likely to be heard. Many coast guard outfits only have a few dozen coast guardsmen assigned to them, meaning recruits will quickly become close with their coworkers and learn how to efficiently get things done as a team. At the same time, the coast guard has by far the lowest budget of any of the armed services.

The work of a coast guardsman is active and strenuous. While a unit might be stationed at a small boat station along the sunny shores of Florida, there is also a chance it could be assigned to a buoy tender in the chilly Alaskan summers. When most people are heading toward shore to avoid a harrowing storm, a coast guardsman's day on the sea may just be getting started.

JOINING THE COAST GUARD

As the smallest armed service in the United States, the coast guard can afford to be selective about its recruits. Coast guard recruiters look for applicants with good high school grades, an aptitude for math and science, and well-rounded extracurricular activities. Applicants for enlisted positions must typically be between the ages of 17 and 27.[1]

Accepted applicants will generally wait between six and eight months before leaving for boot camp. But this is not time to sit by idly and relax. The coast guard's boot camp program is only eight weeks long, and each recruit must meet a rigorous set of physical standards before graduation. Boot camp officials encourage applicants waiting for their start date to exercise and prepare for training before even setting foot on the campus of the US Coast Guard Training Center in Cape May, New Jersey.

BOOT CAMP

Cape May is the only coast guard recruit training center in the nation, and the eight weeks spent here mark the start of life as a coast guardsman. Upon arriving at boot camp, recruits are handed a box lunch, a T-shirt, a pair of sweat pants, and new running shoes. All toiletries are provided, right down to toothbrushes. Recruits immediately undergo a medical and dental exam, receive any necessary immunizations, and get a haircut to meet military regulations.

Boot camp begins at 5:30 a.m. and ends at 10:00 p.m. seven days a week. During the first week of training, recruits learn how to be part of a team and take orders. While this might sound easy, it is often the hardest part of boot camp. Next, recruits learn about military drills and customs as they begin their basic coast guard orientation.

BOOT CAMP PHYSICAL FITNESS GRADUATION REQUIREMENTS

Activity	Time/Distance	Men	Women
Sit-ups	one minute	38	32
Push-ups	one minute	29	15
Running	1.5 miles (2.4 km)	12 minutes, 51 seconds	15 minutes, 26 seconds[2]

After that is practical hands-on training, including learning about firefighting and marksmanship.

Midterm exams are at the end of the fourth week. This is also the time when recruits request particular locations for their first assignments. They find out their assignment during the fifth week as they learn about first aid and how to stand watch.

The rest of the time at boot camp is spent preparing for the first assignment. Before recruits are able to graduate, they must pass both the academic and physical fitness exams. Academic exams cover military law, history, and other subjects. Friends and family are invited to attend the graduation ceremony for one last celebration before recruits head off to their new careers as coast guardsmen.

OFFICER TRAINING

Someone who would like to take on leadership roles within the coast guard can also consider becoming an officer. There are three ways to become an officer: graduating from the Coast Guard Academy, successfully completing Officer Candidate School, or finishing a Direct Commissioning Program.

The Coast Guard Academy was founded in 1876 as a school for the Revenue Cutter Service, and it was actually located on a boat. Today, it is a four-year university located in New London, Connecticut. It emphasizes academics, at-sea training, and leadership development for future coast guard officers. Each year, more than 3,000 high school students apply for one of 300 available spots.[3] Cadets take on a rigorous year-round schedule, with breaks for holidays and a short summer vacation, but the hard work is worth it. At-sea training is done on a ship reserved for that purpose, a sailing vessel called the *Eagle*. Each graduate earns a bachelor of science

The *Eagle* is the only active sailing vessel in US military service.

THE EAGLE

Built in 1936 in Germany, the Eagle is 295 feet (90 m) long and has three masts rigged with 21,350 square feet (1,980 sq m) of sail.[4] While aboard the Eagle, cadets apply their navigation and engineering training and learn how to work together as a crew. All cadets train on the Eagle for a week before their first year of school, with additional opportunities for travel and training during their time at the academy.

The Eagle, originally named Horst Wessel, was once a training vessel for German sailors. The coast guard took possession of the ship in 1945 as a war reparation and renamed it. It has been used as a training vessel at the academy ever since. It is one of only five training barques, or three-masted ships, in the world. The others are in Romania, Portugal, Germany, and Russia.

degree and a commission at the rank of ensign. A commission is the official document given to people who become officers. Tuition for the program is free in exchange for five years of service after graduation.

At only 17 weeks, Officer Candidate School is a much shorter training program. It also takes place in New London, Connecticut. Civilians and current enlisted members looking for leadership opportunities are encouraged to apply. Areas of study include nautical science, law enforcement, seamanship, and leadership. Graduates earn the rank of ensign in the Coast Guard Reserve with an obligation of at least three years of service.

Civilians and coast guard enlisted members with specific experience may apply for the Direct Commission Officer Program. This program fills officer positions in critically

A DAY AT THE UNITED STATES COAST GUARD ACADEMY

6:00 a.m.: Cadets are woken by a bugle call.

6:20 a.m.: At formation, cadets meet with their divisions to catch up with friends and eat breakfast.

7:00 a.m.: Military training period. Cadets take classes, participate in educational events, and get updates on the fleet.

8:00 a.m.: Morning classes. Students take a combination of academic and athletic courses, including cyber defense, detection of nuclear devices, and strategic intelligence, alongside staples such as physics, English, history, and calculus.

12:05 p.m.: Noon formation and lunch.

1:00 p.m.: Afternoon classes. Some are academic, while others are physical. Physical activity is a priority at the academy, not only to prepare cadets for the strenuous jobs they will be undertaking, but also as a platform to develop social relationships with fellow cadets.

4:00 p.m.: Athletic period. The academy offers 30 different sports, including boxing, rowing, and dance.

5:00 p.m.: Evening meal.

7:00 p.m.: Activity hour. Recruits join friends for a club meeting or choir rehearsal, or they relax in the cadet lounge.

8:00 p.m.: Evening study period.

10:00 p.m.: A bugler plays the song *Taps*, a tradition signifying the closing of the day and reminding cadets to reflect on the sacrifices made by others before them.

needed areas, such as aviation, engineering, and intelligence. There are also positions for people who have served as officers in other branches of the military.

Coast guard training programs acquaint students with old-fashioned sailing techniques.

Education and training are just small parts of what it takes to become a valuable member of the US Coast Guard. But not everything can be taught. There are some things coast guardsmen must experience on the job.

NATIONAL MOTOR LIFEBOAT SCHOOL

There are many opportunities for additional career-focused training in the coast guard. One of these takes place near the mouth of the Columbia River in Washington State. Here, at the National Motor Lifeboat School, coast guardsmen from all over the country learn how to use a motor lifeboat in the roughest of conditions.

Extreme winds are normal here, as are massive waves. Half of the training time is spent ashore learning about wave movements and lifeboat maneuvers, but the rest of class is in the water. Trainees are taught proven methods of water rescue, as well as how to tow or deliver salvage equipment to other boats. Most important, they learn the skills and confidence needed to face the sea head on.

CHAPTER NINE
LIFE IN THE COAST GUARD

In an average day, the US Coast Guard answers 100 search and rescue calls, helps 200 people in distress, and saves 10 lives. It also helps contain 20 chemical spills, assists 2,500 vessels entering and leaving the United States, boards 150 vessels, and seizes $10 million in illegal drugs.[1]

The coast guard is headquartered in Washington, D.C.
and divides its responsibilities across nine districts that
encompass the entire United States. The jobs available
to enlisted coast guardsmen who work in these areas are
divided into four distinct groups: the Deck and Ordnance
Group, the Hull and Engineering Group, the Aviation

Group, and the Administrative and Scientific Group. Officers in the coast guard pursue careers that carry with them greater challenges and responsibilities.

DECK AND ORDNANCE GROUP

The Deck and Ordnance Group specializes in jobs relating to the operation of coast guard vessels. Enlisted coast guardsmen in this group have job titles like boatswain's mate, gunner's mate, operations specialist, and intelligence specialist.

Boatswain's mates perform any task related to deck maintenance, small boat operations, and navigation. They supervise everyone assigned to a ship's deck force. They should have strong leadership skills, a knowledge of math, and good physical fitness. Gunner's mates deal with weapons. They use, maintain, and instruct others in all weaponry, so they should be comfortable with mechanics, basic electric theory, and math. They also need to be good at paying attention to detail.

Operations specialists have a wide range of duties, from search and rescue to law enforcement to intelligence operations.

I am a Coast Guardsman.
I serve the people of the United States.
I will protect them.
I will defend them.
I will save them.
I am their shield.
For them I am Semper Paratus.
I live the Coast Guard core values.
I am proud to be a Coast Guardsman.
We are the United States Coast Guard.[2]
    —The Coast Guard Ethos

Intelligence specialists collect, analyze, process, and report information gained in the field. They are required to be US citizens and need to have a top-secret security clearance. This means the person is trusted with secret information. People in these areas should have an interest in computers and communications.

Mergers and reorganizations have left the districts of the US Coast Guard not sequentially numbered.

US COAST GUARD DISTRICTS

DISTRICT 13

DISTRICT 9   DISTRICT 1

DISTRICT 11

DISTRICT 8

DISTRICT 5

DISTRICT 7

DISTRICT 17

DISTRICT 14

N

Damage controlmen are sometimes responsible for operating cutting torches aboard buoy tenders.

HULL AND ENGINEERING GROUP

The Hull and Engineering Group specializes in jobs relating to the upkeep and operation of coast guard vessels. Enlisted coast guardsmen in this group have job titles like damage controlman, electrician's mate, electronics technician, information system technician, and machinery technician.

Damage controlmen fix damage to the ship and maintain emergency equipment. They detect and respond to chemical, biological, and radiological threats. They should have an interest in welding, carpentry, plumbing, and fighting fires.

Electrician's mates install and manage electric and electronic equipment. A strong knowledge of math is required, as is attention to detail. Electronics technicians oversee communications systems, electronic warfare systems, navigation systems, and general electronics systems. Electronics technicians need to excel in mathematics and have an eye for detailed work.

Information system technicians work with the computers that collect, store, process, and forward all voice, data, and video information. Machinery technicians maintain engines, systems that pump fresh air through the ship, and other mechanical parts of the vessel.

AVIATION GROUP

The members of the Aviation Group perform jobs related to the maintenance and operation of coast guard airplanes and helicopters. Coast guardsmen in this group have job titles like avionics electrical technician, aviation maintenance technician, and aviation survival technician.

Avionics electrical technicians maintain and repair all avionics systems. This includes the systems that help aircraft navigate, avoid collisions, lock weapons on to targets, and fly on autopilot. Aviation maintenance technicians troubleshoot all other aircraft systems. Both

RESCUE SWIMMER TRAINING

Rescue swimmers are considered to be among the coast guard's most elite forces. It is not easy to become a rescue swimmer. There have been times when entire classes have dropped out after the first week. The physical requirements—running, swimming, push-ups, sit-ups, pull-ups, and chin-ups—are grueling, helping prepare students for crisis situations in a raging sea.

In addition to the physical aspects of training, rescue swimmer candidates attend classes about the aircraft they will be using and complete four weeks of emergency medical training to learn how to provide basic life support for the people they rescue.

kinds of technicians must qualify for security clearance.

Aviation survival technicians are also known as rescue swimmers, but they have a wide range of duties. They perform search and rescue operations and serve as emergency medical technicians. They also perform the ground handling and servicing of aircraft, including routine aircraft inspection. Aviation survival technicians must be in superior physical condition and qualify for security clearance.

ADMINISTRATIVE AND SCIENTIFIC GROUP

The final group of enlisted coast guardsmen is the Administrative and Scientific Group, which is responsible for providing operations support, conducting environmental inspections, and protecting the health and well-being of coast guard personnel. Coast guardsmen in this group have job titles like food service specialist, health service technician, marine science technician, public affairs specialist, storekeeper, and yeoman.

Food service specialists handle all of the duties associated with feeding a hungry crew, including cooking, baking, sanitation, accounting, purchasing, storage, and dining facility management. They should have knowledge of nutrition, as well as the ability to safely handle food. Health services technicians provide routine and emergency health-care services in large coast guard clinics or small sick bays either ashore or at sea. They must have strong attention to detail and an ability to work closely with others.

Even food service specialists are trained to use a cutter's weapons in case of emergency.

Marine science technicians protect US waters from aquatic nuisance species, supervise the response to spills of dangerous chemicals and other hazardous materials, and examine domestic vessels. Candidates must be detail oriented and flexible.

Public affairs specialists engage in media relations, journalism, web design, photography, video, public speaking, and desktop publishing. Strong communication skills are needed, as is the ability to work in a variety of different media and situations.

Storekeepers are the coast guard's expert purchasing agents, accountants, and property managers. They keep track of supplies and spare parts, and they need superior organizational skills.

Yeomen serve as career and guidance counselors, helping fellow coast guardsmen navigate career moves, retirement options, and incentive programs.

HELP AT HOME

Someone who likes the idea of helping fellow mariners but is not ready to commit to becoming a full-time coast guardsman can instead join the US Coast Guard Auxiliary. As the civilian arm of the coast guard, auxiliary volunteers contribute to the safety and security of US citizens, ports, waterways, and coastal regions. They do this by educating recreational boaters, performing safety patrols in their local areas, and assisting active-duty coast guardsmen with safety inspections, port security, and environmental protection. Some auxiliary members also assist with administrative and technical duties, such as graphic design, photography, and communications.

Yeomen must have excellent interpersonal skills.

COAST GUARD CAREERS

Some careers in the coast guard are open only to officers. These positions require larger amounts of training and carry more responsibilities. One major position reserved for officers is aviation. All coast guard pilots are officers. Officers also take on management positions dealing with computers, finances, logistics, and human resources. Doctors, lawyers, and engineers in the coast guard are also officers.

The coast guard has jobs for just about every personality and every skill set. Coast guardsmen from every division are assigned to posts around the country, and sometimes even around the globe. Since the majority of the coast guard's duties are related to homeland security and US law enforcement, most coast guardsmen are stationed stateside. That can mean working on shore at a small boat

WOMEN IN THE COAST GUARD

Women have played a major role in the coast guard since the days of the Lighthouse Service. That tradition continues today. Unlike other US military forces, there are no positions in the coast guard that cannot be filled by a woman. Approximately 14 percent of all coast guardsmen are women, and they have held every position in the service, including rescue swimmer.[3]

The US Coast Guard Academy was the first service academy to admit women, starting in 1975. Fourteen women from that first class graduated in 1980. Since then, the academy has graduated more than 1,000 women.[4] Today, approximately 30 percent of cadets at the academy are women.[5]

COAST GUARD RANKS

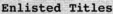

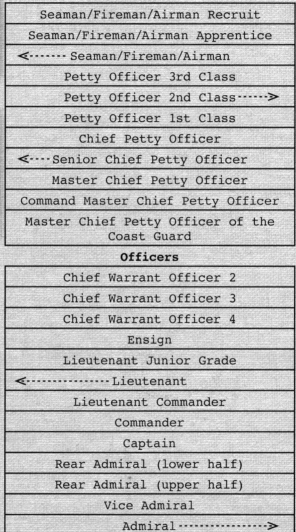

Enlisted Titles

Seaman/Fireman/Airman Recruit
Seaman/Fireman/Airman Apprentice
<-------- Seaman/Fireman/Airman
Petty Officer 3rd Class
Petty Officer 2nd Class ------>
Petty Officer 1st Class
Chief Petty Officer
<----Senior Chief Petty Officer
Master Chief Petty Officer
Command Master Chief Petty Officer
Master Chief Petty Officer of the Coast Guard

Officers

Chief Warrant Officer 2
Chief Warrant Officer 3
Chief Warrant Officer 4
Ensign
Lieutenant Junior Grade
<---------------Lieutenant
Lieutenant Commander
Commander
Captain
Rear Admiral (lower half)
Rear Admiral (upper half)
Vice Admiral
Admiral ---------------->

station, working at a port or harbor, or spending months at a time at sea on an enormous cutter. No matter where a coast guardsman serves, he or she is one of the more than 40,000 men and women who are Semper Paratus—Always Ready.

TIMELINE

1789

The Lighthouse Service is established.

1790

The Revenue Marine Service (later named the Revenue Cutter Service) is established.

1878

The US Lifesaving Service begins.

1912

The *Titanic* sinks.

1915

The Revenue Marine Service and US Lifesaving Service combine to form the US Coast Guard under the Department of the Treasury.

1920–1933

Prohibition is in effect. Coast guardsmen battle against liquor smugglers on the water.

1939

The Lighthouse Service joins the coast guard.

1946

The Bureau of Marine Inspection and Navigation joins the coast guard permanently.

1967

The coast guard moves to the Department of Transportation.

1980

The Mariel Boatlift brings thousands of people from Cuba to the United States.

2003

The coast guard moves to the Department of Homeland Security.

2010

The coast guard responds to the *Deepwater Horizon* oil spill.

ESSENTIAL FACTS

DATE OF FOUNDING
January 28, 1915

MOTTO
Semper Paratus
(Always Ready)

PERSONNEL (2013)
42,000 active duty members
30,000 volunteer auxiliarists
8,700 civilian employees
7,800 reservists

ROLE
The US Coast Guard is one of the United States' five armed forces. Situated in the Department of Homeland Security, the coast guard is responsible for maritime safety and security on US shores and at sea. Its duties include law enforcement, search and rescue, defense readiness, and drug and migrant interdiction. The coast guard is also a steward of the sea, protecting endangered species and US fishing interests and ensuring navigable waterways for trade and commerce.

SIGNIFICANT MISSIONS

Mariel Boatlift, 1980

Exxon Valdez oil spill, 1989

Hurricane Katrina relief, 2005

Deepwater Horizon oil spill response, 2010

WELL-KNOWN COAST GUARDSMEN

Michael Healy led the efforts of the Revenue Cutter Service in Alaska in the late 1800s.

Sumner Kimball, the head of the Treasury Department's Revenue Marine Division, oversaw the creation of the Lifesaving Service in the late 1800s.

Ida Lewis was a member of the Lighthouse Service who saved many lives.

QUOTE

"I am a Coast Guardsman. I serve the people of the United States. I will protect them. I will defend them. I will save them."—*from the Coast Guard Ethos*

GLOSSARY

APTITUDE
Ability to learn or a natural ability.

CAPSIZE
Turn over.

COMMANDEER
To take possession of by force, especially for military purposes.

COMPLIANCE
A readiness or willingness to yield to others.

CONTRABAND
Goods forbidden by law to be owned or to be brought into or out of a country.

CUTTER
Traditionally, a small sailing boat with one mast; in usage by the coast guard, a large armed boat in government service.

GAFF-RIGGED VESSEL
A vessel with a four-cornered sail suspended from a gaff, a pole jutting from a mast.

INDIGENOUS
Produced, growing, or living naturally in a particular region or environment.

INTERDICT
To intercept.

JURISDICTION
The area in which an authority can legally operate.

MARITIME
Of or relating to navigation or commerce on the sea.

MARTIAL LAW
The law applied by military forces in occupied territory or in an emergency.

NAVIGABLE
Water deep and wide enough to permit passage to ships.

POACH
To hunt or fish unlawfully.

REPLICA
A close reproduction of an object.

SURVEILLANCE
Close watch over.

TWEEN DECK
A storage space below the main deck.

ADDITIONAL RESOURCES

SELECTED BIBLIOGRAPHY

Beard, Tom. *The Coast Guard*. New York: Universe, 2010. Print.

Helvarg, David. *Rescue Warriors*. New York: Saint Martin's, 2009. Print.

FURTHER READINGS

Dolan, Edward F. *Careers in the US Coast Guard*. New York: Benchmark, 2009. Print.

Kroll, C. Douglas. *A Coast Guardsman's History of the US Coast Guard*. Annapolis, MD: Naval Institute Press, 2010. Print.

Tougias, Michael J., and Casey Sherman. *The Finest Hours: The True Story of the US Coast Guard's Most Daring Sea Rescue*. New York: Scribner, 2009. Print.

WEBSITES

To learn more about Essential Library of the US Military, visit **booklinks.abdopublishing.com**. These links are routinely monitored and updated to provide the most current information available.

PLACES TO VISIT

BOSTON LIGHT

Boston Harbor

617-223-8666

http://www.bostonharborislands.org/tour-lighthouse

Take a tour of Boston Light, the last remaining US lighthouse operated by the coast guard.

COAST GUARD MONUMENT

Arlington National Cemetery

Arlington, Virginia 22211

877-907-8585

http://www.arlingtoncemetery.mil/visitorinformation/
MonumentMemorials/CoastGuard.aspx

Dedicated on May 23, 1928, this pyramid-shaped white marble monument was built to honor the members of the coast guard who lost their lives in World War I (1914–1918).

SOURCE NOTES

CHAPTER 1. SURVIVING A SUPERSTORM

1. Michael Kruse. "The Last Voyage of the Bounty." *Tampa Bay Times*. Tampa Bay Times, 24 Oct. 2013. Web. 27 Feb. 2014.

2. "Storm Encyclopedia: Hurricanes and Tropical Storms." *Weather.com*. Weather Channel, 2012. Web. 27 Feb. 2014.

3. Michael Kruse. "The Last Voyage of the Bounty." *Tampa Bay Times*. Tampa Bay Times, 24 Oct. 2013. Web. 27 Feb. 2014.

4. "Superstorm Sandy: A Daily Diary." *Weather.com*. Weather Channel, 30 Oct. 2013. Web. 27 Feb. 2014.

5. "Hurricane Sandy: As It Happened." *YouTube/WSJ Digital Network*. Wall Street Journal, 2 Nov. 2012. Web. 27 Feb. 2014.

6. Michael Kruse. "The Last Voyage of the Bounty." *Tampa Bay Times*. Tampa Bay Times, 24 Oct. 2013. Web. 27 Feb. 2014.

7. Stephanie Young. "Shipmate of the Week—Rescuers of the HMS Bounty." *Coast Guard Compass*. US Coast Guard, 2 Nov. 2012. Web. 27 Feb. 2014.

8. Ibid.

CHAPTER 2. ORIGINS

1. "US Coast Guard: A Historical Overview." *US Coast Guard*. US Coast Guard, 26 Nov. 2012. Web. 27 Feb. 2014.

2. David Helvarg. *Rescue Warriors*. New York: St. Martin's, 2009. Print. 60.

3. "US Coast Guard: A Historical Overview." *US Coast Guard*. US Coast Guard, 26 Nov. 2012. Web. 27 Feb. 2014.

4. David Helvarg. *Rescue Warriors*. New York: St. Martin's, 2009. Print. 60.

CHAPTER 3. A NEW BEGINNING

1. David Helvarg. *Rescue Warriors*. New York: St. Martin's, 2009. Print. 73–74.

2. Ibid. 84.

3. R. J. Papp Jr. "US Coast Guard Reserve Policy Statement." *US Coast Guard*. US Coast Guard, n.d. Web. 28 Feb. 2014.

4. "United States Coast Guard 2013 Posture Statement." *US Coast Guard*. US Coast Guard, Apr. 2013. Web. 28 Feb. 2014.

5. "Summary of the DOD Fiscal Year 2014 Budget Proposal." *Department of Defense*. Department of Defense, n.d. Web. 28 Feb. 2014.

6. "United States Coast Guard 2013 Posture Statement." *US Coast Guard*. US Coast Guard, Apr. 2013. Web. 28 Feb. 2014.

CHAPTER 4. A FORMIDABLE FLEET

1. Tom Beard. *The Coast Guard*. New York: Universe, 2010. Print. 214.
2. "Aircraft, Boats, and Cutters." *US Coast Guard*. US Coast Guard, 28 Oct. 2013. Web. 28 Feb. 2014.
3. Tom Beard. *The Coast Guard*. New York: Universe, 2010. Print. 212.
4. Ibid. 201, 212.
5. "National Security Cutter." *US Coast Guard*. US Coast Guard. n.d. Web. 28 Feb. 2014.
6. "Rescue 21 Now Covers Continental US Coastline; Deployment Continues in Alaska and Western Rivers." *US Coast Guard*. US Coast Guard, 28 Nov. 2012. Web. 28 Feb. 2014.
7. Ibid.
8. Tom Beard. *The Coast Guard*. New York: Universe, 2010. Print. 189.
9. "P229." *Sig Sauer*. Sig Sauer, 2013. Web. 28 Feb. 2014.
10. "Aircraft, Boats, and Cutters." *US Coast Guard*. US Coast Guard, 28 Oct. 2013. Web. 28 Feb. 2014.
11. Ibid.
12. Ibid.
13. Ibid.
14. "USCG: About the Acquisition Directorate." *US Coast Guard*. US Coast Guard, 17 Oct. 2013. Web. 28 Feb. 2014.

CHAPTER 5. MARITIME SAFETY

1. "AuxHome." *US Coast Guard Auxiliary*. US Coast Guard, n.d. Web. 28 Feb. 2014.
2. "Frequently Asked Questions." *IMO*. IMO, 2014. Web. 28 Feb. 2014.
3. "About Us." *US Coast Guard*. US Coast Guard, 9 Sept. 2013. Web. 16 Oct. 2013.
4. "Rescue and Survival Systems Manual." *US Coast Guard*. US Coast Guard, 3 Jan. 2007. Web. 28 Feb. 2014.
5. Tom Beard. *The Coast Guard*. New York: Universe, 2010. Print. 314.
6. Ibid. 318.
7. "The US Coast Guard & Hurricane Katrina." *US Coast Guard*. US Coast Guard, 4 Sept. 2013. Web. 28 Feb. 2014.

CHAPTER 6. MARITIME SECURITY

1. Tom Beard. *The Coast Guard*. New York: Universe, 2010. Print. 277–278.

2. Craig Neubecker. "Coast Guard Helicopter Interdiction Tactical Squadron (HITRON-Jacksonville)." *US Coast Guard*. US Coast Guard, 2004. Web. 28 Feb. 2014.

3. "Mariel Boatlift." *GlobalSecurity.org*. Global Security, 2014. Web. 28 Feb. 2014.

4. David Helvarg. *Rescue Warriors*. New York: St. Martin's, 2009. Print. 110.

5. "About Us." *US Coast Guard*. US Coast Guard, 9 Sept. 2013. Web. 16 Oct. 2013.

6. David Helvarg. *Rescue Warriors*. New York: St. Martin's, 2009. Print. 81.

CHAPTER 7. MARINE STEWARDSHIP

1. "US. Coast Guard: America's Maritime Guardian." *US Coast Guard*. US Coast Guard, 1 Jan. 2002. Web. 28 Feb. 2014.

2. Ibid.

3. Tom Beard. *The Coast Guard*. New York: Universe, 2010. Print. 218–219.

4. Ibid. 26, 227.

5. Ibid. 144.

6. "Aircraft, Boats, and Cutters." *US Coast Guard*. US Coast Guard, 28 Oct. 2013. Web. 28 Feb. 2014.

CHAPTER 8. TRAINING

1. "How to Join." *Coast Guard and Coast Guard Reserve*. US Coast Guard, n.d. Web. 28 Feb. 2014.
2. "Training Center Cape May." *US Coast Guard*. US Coast Guard, n.d. Web. 28 Feb. 2014.
3. Tom Beard. *The Coast Guard*. New York: Universe, 2010. Print. 358.
4. "Aircraft, Boats, and Cutters." *US Coast Guard*. US Coast Guard, 28 Oct. 2013. Web. 28 Feb. 2014.

CHAPTER 9. LIFE IN THE COAST GUARD

1. Tom Beard. *The Coast Guard*. New York: Universe, 2010. Print. 203.
2. "US Coast Guard Ethos." *Department of Homeland Security*. Department of Homeland Security, n.d. Web. 28 Feb. 2014.
3. "Coast Guard Snapshot 2012." *US Coast Guard*. US Coast Guard, n.d. Web. 28 Feb. 2014.
4. "Women Leaders of the Coast Guard." *US Coast Guard*. US Coast Guard, n.d. Web. 28 Feb. 2014.
5. "US Coast Guard Academy." *Collegestats.org*. Collegestats.org, 2014. Web. 28 Feb. 2014.

INDEX

ABOUT THE AUTHOR

Kristin Marciniak is a graduate of the University of Missouri-Columbia School of Journalism. She lives in Kansas City, Missouri, with her husband, golden retriever, and very energetic toddler. When she's not writing about United States history, she can be found in her craft room plotting new quilts and untangling miles of yarn.